Table of Contents

Introduction 5

Chapter 1. Challenges of Handling a Disaster Calamity in Urban Setting 6

Chapter 2. Preparing For a Calamity - Things/Foods to Pack 11

Chapter 3. Survival Techniques.. 19

Chapter 4. Things You Must Never Do in Case Of a Calamity 25

Conclusion... 28

Thank You Page.. 29

Survival Guide For Beginners: Essential Preparedness Tips, Techniques and Tactics to Survive in an Emergency or Disaster Situation

By Charles Maldonado

© Copyright 2015 Charles Maldonado

Reproduction or translation of any part of this work beyond that permitted by section 107 or 108 of the 1976 United States Copyright Act without permission of the copyright owner is unlawful. Requests for permission or further information should be addressed to the author.

This publication is designed to provide accurate and authoritative information in regard to the subject matter covered. This work is sold with the understanding that the publisher is not engaged in rendering legal, accounting, or other professional services. If legal advice or other expert assistance is required, the services of a competent professional person should be sought.

First Published, 2015

Printed in the United States of America

Survival Guide For Beginners:

Essential Preparedness Tips, Techniques and Tactics to Survive in an Emergency or Disaster Situation

By

Charles Maldonado

Introduction

All living things, be it humans, animals or plants were born to survive – or at least fight to survive. Even though it is engraved into our very DNA, there are times when it is more of a task than it is of an innate thing. There are times when the weak perish, and the strong emerge to thrive even more in the new environment. With human beings depending on tools for survival, knowing what to pack in case of a calamity and the simple tricks to employ could be the difference between death and life.

Most of the things in the urban setting are manmade. This is why survive in the urban setting is so hard. You will need tools to get nourishment from your immediate settings. Skills in navigation basic are much needed to avoid hiking around in circles. You will need to have the heart and knowledge needed to collaborate with any people you meet to make your survival easier.

Chapter 1. Challenges of Handling a Disaster Calamity in Urban Setting

Natural disasters such as earthquakes and floods can happen anywhere and when they do, they leave behind a trail of destruction. Usually, lives are lost and property of unknown value is often on the line of loss. With the most abrupt shift of human population happening in the world currently, most people are moving for a better life in areas of urban.

If there is any place that such disasters are felt even more it is in the urban areas of major world countries. Even though, when a disaster happens the only remedy is to assist those affected and try to bring things back to normal. In the attempt to do this, rescuers and aid workers are faced with certain challenges unique to urban centers. Some of these challenges are discussed below.

Most world countries experience massive increase in population every hour in their major cities with an average of two people moving to major towns and cities every hour. Although this trend may have a positive impact to the nation's economy because the more urbanized a country is the higher the earnings of its people, it offers a unique challenge when looked at in terms of disaster managements.

The risks brought about by natural disasters including catastrophic fires, landslides, tidal waves and massive floods tend to hit hardest in populous areas. If a city or town happens to bethel culprit then there will be unimaginable loss of property and lives. As the population rises, so will the number of affected victims and lost lives when such disasters strike.

Urban centers are a real maze

In addition, the rapid increase of people in urban centers means that the authorities becomes overwhelmed in managing and setting up protective measures in case of natural calamities. This means that dwellers are left at the mercies of natural disasters due to poor planning and management. Most people will die if anything happens abruptly because of the high vulnerability. This is especially crucial in coastal towns, which also faces rapid population growth.

Most research from affected regions shows that a good number of natural disasters are triggered by over population in urban areas. The pressure exerted on the land is overwhelming and tends to intensify or hasten the speed at which an earthquake or flooding with thunderstorms intensities doubling. There is only one way that the government can prevent such from happening or getting out of hand.

Since controlling urban migration may be impossible, it is crucial that every government invests in and publishes the assessments and risk modeling strategies. Urban dwellers should be informed beforehand in case of any impending dangers from natural occurrences to get out of the trouble zones and move to safety before things get critical. This is the only way that the level of damage to property and especially loss of loves will be controlled. Actual disaster management will be minimized because there are few people to get aid to. Global awareness especially in natural disaster prone urban environments is crucial ad may be the only way to collaboratively prevent disasters around the world through preparedness initiatives.

The government will try, but you need to do something too

Even though the government has the responsibility of disseminating information to the public, it is also responsible for mitigating mass panic. This means that they will hide some information from you. Struggling to know the truth, though soothing, might not save you from danger. Making do with whatever information you have at hand would be the most appropriate way to surviving the catastrophe. Act with the worst case scenario based on what you already got.

In as much as prevention is the best remedy, it is important to deal with the challenges on the ground when the calamity strikes. The challenge with dealing with these disasters in urban areas is the lack of proper relief models because majority of those available are designed for large unpopulated areas.

A good example is construction of refugee camps, which is meant to ease logistical challenges when offering relief to affected victims as well as reduce the rates of crime and violence. This is rather challenging in urban centers because most of the regions are mobile and the rates of crimes are higher making it almost impossible to effectively contain the situation. Stabilizing the region after the effects of a catastrophic calamity is more challenging under these grounds.

The other challenge as experienced by disaster responders in most cities and town is the difficulty in implementing coherent camp structures. Unlike the expected, relief providers are forced to make relief camps anywhere there is a small gathering as most people tend together around their former homes. This means that camps are scattered all over the disaster struck region making it almost impossible to provide services than when the camp is in one areas that is designated and accessible to all victims.

Chapter 2. Preparing For a Calamity - Things/Foods to Pack

The wise thing to do when you come from a disaster prone region is to be on the lookout for any possible signs. You need to be vigilant and hid to any warnings from national radio and television stations because these broadcasters usually receive the first warnings, as they are the easiest way to reach majority of residents.

In the event of such announcements, one needs be prepared and ready to be on the move if it calls for it. For this reason, packing an emergency kit can be considered the most appropriate action. You may have to separate the personal supplies and foods you need to survive until everything gets back to normal. This brings into view the notion of the ideal survival kit. The idea of the survival kit that should always be ready at hand in your house and the simple backpack you will piece up once the call comes by.

Have an emergency kit ready

An emergency kit can come in handy for any person in a disaster prone region. You need to know what you must bring and what you need to leave behind no matter how precious it may be to you. Prioritize the things that will be helpful for your immediate needs before everything stabilizes. Start by identifying things that you will need to use, as these must be contained in your kit.

Mold your kit to meet the calamity's problems

Some tutorials would tell you to pack a flashlight, a blanket, coins for pay phones as you will need to communicate at some point to either call for help or give your location, small bills, portable water and a knife among other things. It is important to remember that during an earthquake, flood or any their disaster it is not only important to pack but also to unpack. While this is quite a comprehensive list, the relevance of each item depends on your immediate environment. Coins, for instance would be useless in a modern town without phone booths. Choosing to carry some bleach or mild chlorine to purify water on the go could be a simpler and more viable way to making your luggage lighter.

Never forget the first-aid kit

The other crucial thing to do is to have a first aid kit on standby or make one if it does to exist. Chances of being hurt through cuts and burns while scampering to safety are very high. While getting any medical attention at such times may be a far-fetched dream, the only way to keep you and your loved ones alive for proper medical attention later n is to have a medical first aid kit with you. This kit should contain basic supplies that can help prevent infections and alleviate pain even if it is just shortly.

The moment the warnings are released make sure that you scan your region for hazard areas that must be avoided under all circumstances. It helps to contact your local emergency manager and find out exactly what areas you must not get into when fleeing or if you most then you should at least have a kit that prepares you to survive through it. This could include having flashlights and radios that you can use to communicate and get around especially if it is underground tunnels.

Self-powered portable radios and light

It is important to purchase self-powered flashlights and radios. You do not want to run out of batteries in the event of a disaster when you need to communicate and see where you are. You can also get a satellite phone that will not fail you no matter where you are. Most importantly, you need to pack according to your location. Different things might be needed for emergency based on where you live. Prioritize on the things that you must have regardless of your location.

Navigation tools and skills

A map is essential to carry as this is what will help you get to the nearest evacuation camps when you need to. A signal flare is also important, as it is what will alert rescue teams of your location especially if you are incapable of getting to the rescue centers for one reason or another. Most importantly though, consider your mind as your greatest survival kit. Be careful what you listen to and allow getting to you. Avoid letting over hyped media messages scare you and do what you must to survive.

While reading a map would give you a general idea of your location, having a compass or the basic navigation skills will confirm your physical location. If you cannot find a compass, use the stars and the sun to navigate. Learning how to tell your north with respect to these celestial bodies should make your navigation easier. An alternative would be learning a couple of landmarks like hills and mountains in your area beforehand. You might need this when disaster strikes.

With a pack of the most import things you must get the next sensible thing to do is to pack a bag of food just in case you may have to depart your home due to the effects of the calamity. It is also crucial to have a stack of food ready especially if you are going to be trapped indoors. Chances are that an emergency is not likely to cut you food supply immediately, at least not until two weeks are over. You need not take any chances though as you should prepare a stack that lasts longer and f possible a month or more. You never know whom you may have to feed before any help gets to you.

Some food and water

As such, work on building your food stack. The easiest way to do this is to increases the quantity of what you already have on the shelves keep away from foods rich in proteins and high fat especially if you have a low water supply in addition to not stocking salty foods that get you thirsty fast.

Furthermore, familiar food has a way of boosting morale during stressful times such as calamities. You should look at the possibilities of getting canned foods that will not require any cooking or special preparation that you will be unable to do during the situation you find yourself in. when packing food for the entire family consider their tastes and unique needs as this will help ease the stress of the moment. Your general goal should be to pack tasty food that is has high calories, proteins, carbohydrates, vitamins and minerals.

Your firs trick should be to pack a three day supply of non-perishable food and water just in case you may have to move and leave everything else behind. Keep this stash in a handy place ready for moving in case there is no time to get to collect supplies from the kitchen when the disaster strikes. Choose foods that require no preparation, those that are light in weight and those foods that can be stored easily. If it is necessary to heat food then a can of cooking fuel will be essential. Salt free crackers, whole grains and foods with a lot of water will be most useful during this period.

Consider packing highly recommended foods for disasters. These should include ready to eat canned meats, fruits and vegetables, canned juice, soup and milk, high-energy foods such as crackers, peanut butter, granola bars and jelly. You can also pack comfort foods such as hard candy, sweetened cereals, cookies and candy bars. Instant coffee bags and tea bags also come in handy in addition to special foods for infants, elderly and persons with special diets.

High energy snacks might be the best

You can also consider packing compressed food bars as long as they are lightweight, nutritious and taste good. Trail mixes that are available either as pre-packaged or self-assembled are also a great disaster meal idea. Pack dried foods although they should be your last option because they promote thirst, which is the same to freeze dried foods.

Instant meals, snack sized canned goods and prepackaged beverages are other food alternatives that come in handy during calamities. Avoid commercially dehydrated foods because of their preparation requirements, bottled foods as they are bulky and easy to break, meal sized canned foods because of their weight, and finally whole grains and pastas that involved complicated preparation that may not be possible under the circumstances.

Chapter 3. Survival Techniques

Natural disasters come as a reminder that no one is exempt from natural calamities and effects of nature. Nature is not discriminative. It will not consider where you live. The only way to lessen the brunt of nature's destructions is to be well prepared for it especially if you are in a calamity prone region. Nature's antics are devastating and come in different forms including tornadoes, hurricanes, heat waves, floods, earthquakes, landslides, wild fires, tsunamis and volcanic eruptions just to mention a few. As much as it is human nature to avoid bad news, the tendency of procrastination also exists. Unfortunately, avoiding bad news is not helpful in times of disaster strikes as the only thing that can save a life is being well prepared. You need to have strategies and tactics in place especially if you are in an urban setup where relief is not easy to execute. Luckily, you do n have to wait for things to get this far when you can do something about it before.

Burying your head in sand and waiting for the government to rescue you is no strategy. While most people consider leaving their homes when disasters strike, in some cases this may not be possible because of external factors that make your home a safer haven despite its risk especially when the utilities to get to safety get ripped off. When this happens, it is helpful to bug in and make do with what you have. Your stay can only be possible if you prepared and strategized for it. The following tips should come in handy for any urban dweller in a calamity prone region.

While the government thinks you should prep for three days before help gets to you in a adversity situation, the most reasonable duration should be a minimum of two weeks. In as much as your government may be willing to rescue you within the three days, chances are that it may be impossible to get this done. However, the issue of timing should not act as a hindrance when you have to do what you must. Start with the basic human requirements, which are shelter, food, water, first aid, and self-defense. All these will be crucial when covering yourself from the aftermaths of a natural calamity.

It is only during a calamity situation that you realize there is more to shelter than having a roof over your heads. Shelter should be able to protect you from elements even if access to modern utilities is nonexistent. The first priority when considering shelter is to shield yourself from the cold. Prepare to have alternative heating sources when a disaster strikes in the cold weather. This means therefore that you should have alternative fuel such as wood, kerosene heaters, and portable propane heaters. Make sure that the moment you start hearing warning alerts that you decide on your alternative heating source, purchase it and install. Make sure that you test it to determine the amount of fuel you need during the period that you will be hidden and stick as much fuel as is necessary.

Water is essential for human survival. Droughts are the most common calamities that affect water supply. Dependence on municipal water supply and well sources may not cut it during such situations. In addition, abrupt natural disasters like earthquakes and floods make water scarcity to rise due to the contamination that occurs. You are not cleared to drink floodwater due to the numerous infection risks. In-bug in strategy that may work to resolve this dilemma is to store water in two liters pop bottles.

Using the soap wash the bottles and then with water sanitize the bottles and bleach them. After rinsing and filling them up with clean water you can be assured that this is a safe means of storing water for up to two years which is more than you will need before a disaster rescue team gets to you.

You may need to have fire for warmth or cooking. However, during emergencies choosing foods that require no preparation is the best alternative. Even so, you need to have an alternative place to prepare your meals. This means that you should find affordable alternative means to help with the cooking and boiling of water. Wood burning stoves can be very helpful and all you need to fist is the boiled water should be installed and at the same time it should be cooked. Camping stoves are also another alternative for this problem. The important thing is to choose an alternative that is effective and budget friendly.

Food is the other concern when trapped in after natural calamities strike. The food supply depends on a number of things on normal occasions. Most of these sources are destroyed when calamity strikes making it impossible to access foods. You do not have to worry about lacking food in stores when you are well prepared. The moment the warning signs begin make a point of stoking your shelves with food. Think of pen and eat meals that are ready to consume as they are bought form the stores. You are probably not going to have enough time or the means to prepare food when power is cut.

On the same note, avoid sticking fresh vegetables that will go bad in a few days same to frozen foods. Keep your food storage and meal options simple. If you can get your hands on military meals ready to eat then you, have an even better chance to survive the calamity meal-wise. Canned goods are also great survival meals that you should consider stoking in case of a disaster alert. The good thing with these meals is that they can be eaten cold and direct form the can and no preparation is required.

First aid is crucial when preparing for post calamity survival. You are likely to be injured when running away to safety. Pack an emergency kit that contains pain drugs and other fist aid items such as bandages and sanitizers that may be needed to dress a wound. If you have to talk to your doctor about prescription drugs then make sure, you do so before the disaster strikes.

You need to take the necessary defense measures to protect yourself and your home. Disasters have a way of bringing out the worst in people as it creates an abnormal circumstance. As people fight for the available resources, there is bound to be violence, which you do not want to be part of. Put in place strategies to keep empowered criminals away from your loved ones.

Chapter 4. Things You Must Never Do in Case Of a Calamity

With the challenges that are likely to be faced when calamity strikes and possible strategies to shield yourself from the aftermath, it is also crucial to understand what not to do during and after a disaster. This will depend on the type of calamity in question.

The effect being that you cannot avoid natural disasters, your only chance to survive is minimize its effects on you. This is why you need to take precautions especially concerning travelling. Avoid going towards areas that are disaster prone at certain times of the year. Getting insurance is also a good way to protect your property against damage as well as communicating with the disaster management team on the other end could save you a great deal of trouble. Always notify someone that you are travelling just in case you the disaster happens when you are visiting.

You should not panic when a disaster happens. It is important to remain levelheaded and understand that nothing is working as it should and that you are not the only one being affected by the turn out of events. In fact, getting hysterical is only going to make things worse. You will not be thinking straight and could contribute to the chaos without even being aware of it. Instead, remain calm and get word to your people as soon as you get working communication lines.

Never ignore evacuation orders. Sometimes the magnitude of a disaster is so severe that victims and survivors require immediate evacuation. When this is needed, do not stay back or refrain from getting this assistance for whatever reason, chances are that experts anticipate the situation getting worse especially if it is flooding. The best shot of rescuing you could be resting with the evacuation team.

Do not stand near tall objects that are likely to collapse especially of the natural disaster is an earthquake. The unstable grounds caused by seismic movements have a tendency of weakening building foundations and making trees loose. This exposes you to more risk and danger thus the need to stay clear of tall objects as their stability is even more affected. Avoid damaged structures in earthquakes and floods. About its structures and you are some kind of curious about it especially after the serious damage caused by floods and earthquakes. Assess the situation and plan your exit. It is advisable to meet you family, co-workers, and friends in designated safe areas and await further communication from rescuers.

Never walk in moving water no matter how shallow you think it is. There is a lot of force that comes with moving water and making the mistake of waling in it will push you to grounds that are more dangerous and can even cost your life.

Conclusion

Even though you might be ever ready and full packed in preparation for a calamity, having the wrong people around you could be your very demise. Since you will need partners and friends to survive a calamity, encouraging your family, colleagues and friends to learn a few things about surviving an urban calamity will make you more secure in case disaster strikes.

Thank You Page

I want to personally thank you for reading my book. I hope you found information in this book useful and I would be very grateful if you could leave your honest review about this book. I certainly want to thank you in advance for doing this.

If you have the time, you can check my other books too.

www.ingramcontent.com/pod-product-compliance
Lightning Source LLC
LaVergne TN
LVHW021748060526
838200LV00052B/3546